Between Grace and Grit

Between Grace and Grit

Echoes from the Past

By

RAY CUESTER COMBS

foreword by Cindy Combs

RESOURCE *Publications* • Eugene, Oregon

BETWEEN GRACE AND GRIT
Echoes from the Past

Resource Publications
An Imprint of Wipf and Stock Publishers
199 W. 8th Ave., Suite 3
Eugene, OR 97401

www.wipfandstock.com

PAPERBACK ISBN: 979-8-3852-7141-2
HARDCOVER ISBN: 979-8-3852-7142-9
EBOOK ISBN: 979-8-3852-7143-6

VERSION NUMBER 01/29/26

For Mom and Dad—
who taught us what strength sounds like in a steady voice, a faithful hymn, and lives rooted deep in farm soil and carried far on railroad lines.

Dad's heart grew tired first, yet Mom's reflections during her own cancer journey became a final lesson in courage—light she kept sharing even as the road narrowed. Her example never wavered.

For Lee—my brother in the keeping of memory.

For Pam—gone too soon on a path too familiar,
yet still part of our circle of love.

And for the grandchildren and extended family—may you continue to walk the long tracks and tend the rich fields they laid out before us with such grace, grit, and goodness.

How you look at life shapes how you walk through it. Stay positive, stay hopeful, and life becomes a bowl of cherries—not perfect, not always easy, but manageable, even joyful, when things go wrong. Be flexible. Keep going when plans fall apart. And when they do—try again.

~Elsie Hunter Combs

Contents

Foreword

BY CINDY COMBS

History has no clear beginning and no end, but in this narrative of a family's story—detailing the impact of its leadership and direction as it responds to events and challenges—we gain insight into moments many of us have lived through. This flowing narrative is not an historical account of events; rather, it offers a compelling portrait of a family's life as the nation wrestles with racism in the turbulent 1960s and 1970s. Led by the parents, Bob and Elsie Combs, this family became living examples of the "grit and grace" needed to navigate a changing world, shaping their community even as they guided their own children.

Bob Combs, ordained as a Presbyterian minister in North Carolina, had the "grit" to work openly with the NAACP to advocate for fair elections and integration in schools and workplaces—an unpopular and often dangerous stance in the South during the 1960s. The author's account of the stress and threats faced in their home and schools reflects the harsh realities of the era. Yet it also reveals the quiet "grace" embodied by Elsie, whose steady love and caregiving helped the family endure and ultimately return to North Carolina, closer to their extended kin.

Through this narrative, anyone who lived or worked through the upheavals of the 1970s will recognize the familiar tensions. As civil rights activism merged with the struggle for gender equality, Bob Combs's role as pastor of Sweetwater Presbyterian Church in Hickory, North Carolina, grew even more demanding when he was elected to the state senate. His "grit" in representing his constituents while remaining true to his convictions is evident in his work on challenging issues, including equal rights for women.

At the same time, Elsie's "grace"—teaching science, completing her master's degree at Appalachian State University, serving the faith community, and leading Presbyterian Women—left a lasting imprint on their children, who saw her not only as "Mom," but as a quiet force for good.

This narrative offers a richly felt reflection on how a family's leaders faced the pressures of their world with determination and compassion. Most of us can name the adults who shaped our understanding of life. Ray Combs's carefully crafted and well-researched memoir, grounded in family archives and lived memory, invites readers to revisit their own stories, their own formative influences, and the world they inherited. More should do what Ray has done: preserve these memories and insights so that we might learn—together—how we became who we are.

Dr. Cindy Combs
Author of *Terrorism in the Twenty-First Century* (nine editions);
Encyclopedia of Terrorism (two editions);
and contributor to numerous books and articles on terrorism

Preface

Between Grace and Grit

This book began as a collection of stories—small moments I carried for decades, bits of memory that surfaced during long drives, quiet mornings, or while sorting through boxes of family photographs. I never intended to write a memoir. I simply wanted to understand the shape of the lives that shaped me.

As I wrote, the story widened. What began as my parents' narrative—Bob and Elsie Combs, two steadfast people who believed faith should move and justice should mean something—became a broader reflection on the places we lived and the times we endured. Norfolk during early desegregation. Richmond in the heat of political resistance. Sweetwater community, Hickory, where community and conflict shared the same roads. My childhood unfolded at the intersection of family, history, and a region undergoing painful but necessary change.

I grew up inside that swirl—inside the parsonage, inside the politics, inside the tension between appearance and truth. Everyone had an opinion about the preacher's kids, and I knew the script before I knew myself. As a young PK, I often lived up to the billing—halo one minute, mischief the next. I wasn't rebellious so much as restless, learning early how thin the line could be between expectation and becoming. Much of the rhythm in these pages comes from that tension: a boy absorbing lessons faster than he understood them, an adult circling back to make sense of what he carried for decades.

These chapters move between memory and moment, between a child's view and an adult's understanding. The rhythm is intentional. Much of life in our home was set to a kind of cadence—sermons and schoolbooks, hymns and headlines, Mom's quiet strength and Dad's determined fire. To tell the story straight would be to flatten what was textured. So I let the voice shift, sometimes poetic, sometimes plainspoken, depending on how the memory still feels in my hands.

This is not a historical record, though it is rooted in real events, letters, photographs, and family archives. It is a son's reconstruction—honest about perspective, aware that memory carries both clarity and shadow. Where details blur, the emotion remains steady, anchored by the lessons my parents lived more than taught.

I wrote this book to honor them but also to understand the legacy they left: that grace can hold its ground and grit can still be gentle; that faith and justice are not opposing forces; and that a life of purpose often begins in ordinary rooms with extraordinary people.

If the reader finds echoes of their own story here—of family, of struggle, of becoming—then the writing has done its work.

—Ray Cuester Combs

Acknowledgments

This book was carried forward by far more than memory. It was held together by the people who shaped my life with their presence, their guidance, and their love.

To my parents, Bob and Elsie Combs—your faith, courage, and compassion built the tracks I rediscovered. Every chapter here bears your fingerprints. Your lives were the first stories I ever learned to trust.

To my brother, Lee, for his thoughtful insight, steady support, and the ways he helped me remember not only the events but the meaning behind them. And to the memory of my sister, Pam, whose quiet strength and fierce spirit remain part of every step forward.

To my extended family across the Hunter and Combs lines—their photographs, keepsakes, and recollections became touchstones that grounded this narrative. Special thanks to those who shared stories, letters, and fragments of the past that helped this book take shape.

My gratitude also extends to the teachers, preachers, neighbors, civil rights leaders, public servants, and community advocates who moved through our lives in Hickory, Richmond, Norfolk, and beyond. Your influence echoes throughout these pages.

To the early readers of this manuscript, whose thoughtful suggestions sharpened its focus and deepened its rhythm—thank you for helping me hear what the story needed.

And finally, to my family—children, grandchildren, and those who have welcomed me into their lives. Your belief in this project reminded me why the story matters. May the grace and grit you see in these pages continue to guide us all.

Prologue

Between Grace and Grit

I didn't write this to rewrite history.
I wrote it to remember—
my parents,
the voices that shaped me
before I understood what shaping meant.

They weren't perfect,
but they were steady.
Relentless.
Powerful.

Their love didn't parade.
It showed up—
in casseroles and campaign trails,
in chalk dust and choir robes,
in Scripture lived out loud,
in science whispered through slides.

Two people
with fire in their bellies
and faith in their bones,
who stood in pulpits and PTA meetings,
who walked into rooms where they weren't wanted
because justice told them to.

Theirs was never a story of spotlights or statues.
It was a steady flame,
carried through the long march toward justice.
They didn't labor for plaques
or for names carved in stone.
They worked for tomorrow,
glancing back only to learn—
never to linger.

Not louder than others.
Not greater than many.
But still:
a fraction of the fight,
a thread in the fabric,
woven with faith,
worn by love.

And me?
I was the tagalong—
a preacher's kid,
a principal's kid.
Privileged.
A witness.
A wanderer.

I shattered the PK mold like glass.
Too curious.
Too mouthy.
More sarcasm than Scripture.

I didn't grasp the weight they carried—
through congregational fractures,
through threats,
when crosses burned,
when marbles shattered our front door.
When fire met fire,
fear met defiance.

When politics split the air,
cutting through pews and pulpits,
dividing families at the table—
voices raised,
silence louder still,
neighbors turned to sides.

I do now.

Now I see what they built—
a home that held us
and held a line.
A ministry that didn't preach love,
but practiced it—
even when it hurt.
They believed silence was surrender.
And they refused to be silent.

I tried to live my own story,
as if theirs wasn't stitched into my skin.
I lingered in the corners,
half watching,
half listening,
missing more than I knew.

But time softens what once seared.
Loss reveals what always glowed.

So I return—
not to sanitize,
not to sanctify,
but to testify,
from their shadows.

To let their light shine—
not as halos,
but as lanterns.
Stained, sacred,
casting warmth into places—
I still don't understand.

This is their story.
What they gave.
What it cost.
What it changed.

And how it still leads me—
through grit,
through grace,
through the memory
of a love that never let go.

I

Fire and Foundation

I come from quiet fire—
faith with dirt under its nails,
dreams wrapped in denim and gospel.
My story began before I knew how to carry a name—
with two minds that met
in the heat of debate.
Mom and Dad weren't a fairytale;
they were forged in sharp wit
and sharpened hearts.

He stepped into college
his senior year of high school.
Campus life and a command of clubs.

She was awarded Miss Wingate runner-up—
grace without vanity,
wit without pretense—
her mind,
salutatorian's edge,
steady conviction,
kept him leaning closer.

He brought quick humor,
she brought challenge.
She wasn't swayed.

And in that stand,
he found his match—
not just a partner,
but a compass,
a spark of calling
that would carry them,
far beyond Wingate's walls.

Dad came from polished shoes
and unspoken rules—
the son of Custer (CUE-ster) Combs,
a railroad man,
and Vivian Combs,
who corrected grammar mid-sentence.
A world where reputation outweighed truth,
where Bobby Combs had to grow into Robert Lee Combs
just to be taken seriously.

Mom—Elsie Hunter—came from Depression grit.
Her father, Ray, lost his grocery store
because kindness outweighed profit,
then carried strength into the shipyards
and onto a farm.
Her mother, Sadie, raised four kids
with a spine of steel
and hands that never flinched.

Her parents' creed—"Education is your ticket"—
led Mom to college,
to a red '42 Chevy,
to a man with charm and conviction.

They spread a picnic along Catawba's bank.
The river shimmered,
a railroad bridge rose in the distance—
iron ribs against the sky.

There, he asked.
She said yes.
Their "yes" gathered strength,
like the river reshaping itself into Lake Norman—
a reservoir of love
deep enough to carry generations.

They married on Friday the 13th—
not out of fear, but resolve.
Then came their first son.
Dad named him Jr., declared himself Sr.,
ruffled feathers with the name Robert Lee.

Davidson sharpened him.
Union Seminary cracked him open.
He wasn't chasing wealth anymore—
he was chasing God.
Presbyterian to the core,
anchored in McCoy lineage
that stretched back to Scottish stone,
stubborn and steadfast.

Richmond became their launchpad—
a creaky seminary apartment,
a baby soothed while Scripture was studied,
Mom foraging greens behind the building.
Neighbors left food out of pity—
but she was remembering,
not scavenging.

Richmond's smoke ghosted the air—
history refusing to burn away.

In that small place, life flourished:
Robert Jr., then Pam.
No vacations. No rest.

Just work, faith, and love—
ragged, but unbroken.

A church called.
They packed the car—
two little ones,
no money,
a map marked—
running more on faith than fuel.

Plymouth, North Carolina.
Pulp mill smoke,
a diverse community,
a place where an ironclad dream
could just as easily sink.

Presbyterian Church of Plymouth.
The congregation welcomed them
with small gifts—pots, pans, quilts—
like farmers trading seeds,
trusting it might grow.

Dad believed civic duty
was ministry in motion.
He joined the Jaycees,
the Lions Club,
the Boy Scouts District Committee.
Not résumé lines—
strands of calling,
tracks in the ground,
meant to carry others forward.

"A minister," he said,
"should take a vital interest
in the civic enterprises
of the community he serves."

This chapter?
It's about two people—
calloused hands, stubborn hope—
carving something sacred out of struggle.

From their fire,
purpose was forged.
And out of that flame
came us.

2

Where the Water Met the Fire

They left Plymouth before I was born—
before I became the surprise
planted in their next chapter.

It was the four of them:
Mom, Dad, my brother, my sister—
leaving behind a faithful congregation
for something larger, unknown.

Norfolk was next.
A city of sirens and ships,
streets restless with the rising tide
of the Civil Rights Movement.
The moving truck—stuck in the mud.
Life was turning into future sermons,
"Getting the Best of Life by Making Failures Fruitful."

They first settled in a small two-bedroom house,
then into a red-brick manse
on the Elizabeth River.
From a distance, it looked like peace.
But even peace has a current.

One day it swallowed a neighbor child—
no sound, no goodbye,

only silence.
Grief lingered,
but Dad answered it the only way he knew—
with his hands.

He built a boat by hand,
steady as his love,
quiet as his sermons.
It sat on the lawn—
until it was ready to launch,
a lesson in patience,
a vessel of calm.

Norfolk wasn't still.
Not in the streets.
Not in the sanctuary.
Desegregation had come,
and the school board resisted—
church academies
raised to keep Negro children out,
the word spoken freely then,
a reminder now of how language itself
can carry the weight of a wound.

Dad said no.
Not here.
Not under God's name.
That was the Norfolk I was born into.
Not just a city—
a stand.

I was the "accident,"
the extra slice of cake.
Ray—simple, strong,
bound to legacy.
The house by the river became memory:

laughter on hardwood,
storms on the horizon.
Not perfect,
but full of love.

Outside, the world wrestled
with who it wanted to be.
Even I, too young to name it,
would feel the pull.

Dad was preacher in the pulpit
and voice at the podium—
justice, equality, hope,
drawn straight from the Gospels.
His words could stir a crowd,
not for applause but for awakening.

In uncomfortable times he preached
"I Can Accept Your Christ, but Not Your Christianity"—
the kind of truth that turned heads
and opened hearts,
a sermon ahead of its time.

Mom lived the Beatitudes—
not recited,
but walked.
In 1961 she gathered supplies
for the good-will tour,
the Amity III,
bound for Africa's ports.
A photograph shows her on the *USS Donner*,
rooted in Norfolk,
yet linked to distant shores.

Dad, too, reached outward—
helping send medical supplies

to Japan, Korea, Free China, Congo.
Doctors donated,
faith carried them farther
than any pulpit could.

Together their witness stretched
from waters' edge
to distant shores,
proving love of neighbor
knows no borders.

At home, Dad helped plant
a childcare program at Squires Church—
a seed of what community could be.

And me?
Next came schoolyards,
soap punishments,
and lessons in injustice.

But for now, there was Norfolk—
where the river breathed,
where my father found stillness,
and his storm.
Where my mother stood with grace
and guided the boat
through deeper waters.

3

A Tidewater Beginning

Norfolk was where I first heard the world—
not only voices close to me,
but echoes of what might be.

My father baptized me—
water in his hands,
a vow between heaven and earth.
My mother wrapped it all—
faith, family, us—
in Scripture, song, and steady grace.

My earliest memories
weren't protests or pulpits,
but blankets tucked tight,
my brother's trumpet,
my sister's piano keys,
Mom at the mixing bowl.

It felt like love in that house—
brick, river,
Sunday pot roast kind of love.
I was the baby,
the tagalong,
a king in a kingdom of crumbs,
too small to see the storm

already breaking around us.

Dad wrestled with the urgency
of Christian witness in the city.
In Chicago he found clarity:
"The Church cannot minister
if she will not live among the people,
if she will not face
their work, their race, their struggle."

While the world outside came undone,
my parents wrapped me in safety.
Lee carried the oldest burdens,
Pam answered with music.
The spotlight moved between them,
testing us all.

We stayed when leaving
might have been easier.
Stayed when it cost whispers,
stares, and closed doors.

Lee and Pam walked into desegregated schools
with conviction in their book bags.
Mom packed lunches with prayer,
hoping grace could soften
what history had hardened.

Me?
I stayed home with Louise—
Lincoln Logs and crayons,
TV glowing in sunlit rooms,
free to be,
because they were out there
holding the line.

The house held rhythm—
sled rides behind the '57 Chevy,
grandparents' visits,
crafts and sermons.

Tension drifted in from Grandmother Combs,
but Mom had her sister Helen—
a tether across the river,
comfort close at hand.

Romper Room and Gumby
bookended my mornings.
But music filled our home.
It was her inheritance—
a family of voices certain as Sunday.
Her mother sang and played piano.
Her father sang,
her sisters Helen and Susan too.

Harmony was in their blood,
passed like Scripture,
woven like prayer.

Mom's voice rose on hallelujahs,
joined by Helen's,
lifting choirs, steadying hymns,
pouring through thresholds and sanctuaries.

Together they carried it outward—
to concerts, to choirs,
even to the International Music Festival,
where their voices rose with others,
Norfolk's sound turned global,
praise turned to melody,
faith given wings.

Work stretched wide.
Mom poured herself into music,
neighbors, need.
Dad into ministry,
people, place.
Both gave more than they kept.

Even at the Auto Plant,
Dad sought understanding,
bridging faith and labor,
joining leaders to honor
the people who kept the plant alive.

Then—Kennedy was gone.
The TV cut through Mom's ironing.
I didn't understand,
but I remember the silence—
as if the sun had been switched off.

That's when I learned:
grief doesn't always wail.
Sometimes,
it settles.

4

Kryptonite and Quiet Heroes

The Civil Rights Movement pressed into Norfolk.
Lines were drawn—
at City Hall, on school boards,
and in the sanctuary where Dad preached.

My parents stood firm—
marching with neighbors,
speaking truth where silence had settled.

Inside our home,
the static grew louder than the music.
Dad had built a persona—
measured, commanding—
armor for unstable times.

He chased shiny toys—
especially cars.
The Ford Falcon was his prize:
CB radio humming,
whip antenna dancing—
like he was surf-fishing,
casting for connection.

That radio became a lifeline.
One night, a man called in despair.

Mom answered—
steady through the static—
she reached for Dad on the CB,
her voice a bridge between them.
"Talk to him," she said.
And through that hum of wires,
hope traveled.
The man chose to live.
Not in fire,
not in thunder—
but in a still, steady voice.

The Falcon carried us too—
until a backfire set the hood aflame.
Dad doused it with sand.
Like a beachside firefighter.
Trip over.
Story intact.

Mom returned to Old Dominion part time.
I started preschool.
A harsh teacher ruled with soap and ruler.
Her classroom colder
than the white block building that held it.

Then my parents realized
she bristled at the justice
they were trying to build.
Fortunate case of chickenpox—
and home again,
wrapped in warmth.

Family stretched across two states.
At the Hunters' farm—
cows, shiny buckets, and cats
in their daily communion.

Shucking corn,
snapping peas
beneath the old oak tree.
Churning ice cream
as daylight gave way to glow.

At the Combs's home—
trains, stories, storms.
Granddaddy and I on the porch,
watching lightning split the sky.
Grandmother sounding the weather alarm—
"Custer, you boys get in this house!"
Storms came in many forms.
Some slammed doors,
some smiled through silence.
But the storm got in either way.

For Dad, the church was heartbeat—
not only in sermons,
but in soil and sunlight.
He believed even the sanctuary plants,
the flowers by the door,
the tended landscape outside
were part of worship.
Every bloom, every branch
was "a living sermon."

Mom shared that vision.
She brought children close to creation—
on field trips,
in reading circles,
in gardens where small hands touched the earth.
She planted wonder like seeds,
trusting it would grow well beyond the classroom.

But inside, Dad cracked.
Not in sermons,
but in silence.
Fractures in church.
Family tension.
His mother's disapproval.

Then—he slipped.
A bar.
A drink.
Kryptonite.

Even strong men falter.
Even prophets faced their wilderness.
Dad's came with neon lights and quiet withdrawal.

Lee watched over us
as Mom rose.
She pulled him back—
not with anger,
but with resolve.

The fight over segregated academies returned.
Dad refused.
The toll was clear.
The fire dimmed.
But Mom held him steady.

Others noticed his strength.
The Human Relations Council.
Black leaders in Norfolk.
Richmond too.

A new opportunity,
a fresh start.
Not peace,
but new purpose.

The warning came from past leadership:
"Too many localities still resist compliance
with the Civil Rights Act of '64."
It wasn't a farewell.
It was forecast.
Dad was stepping into a storm.

Me?
I was growing up in a house
where quiet heroism
carried more weight than words.
Even then,
I must have felt it.
Because I carry it still.

5

A Calling in the Fire

Our Superman had fallen—
but he rose again,
through grit, grace,
and Mom's steady arms.

He stepped back into the light—
his cape frayed,
but conviction strong enough
to carry him forward.

This was Richmond,
not a 1947 radio episode—
fiery crosses burned for real.
Hate wore suits,
passed out flyers,
preached from pulpits.

Dad walked straight into it.
He answered a call:
to lead the Virginia Council on Human Relations,
to confront racism head-on.

We left Norfolk behind
and drove into the Movement.
Richmond waited—

monuments of bronze,
shadows long.
Children slipped into integrated schools.

A newspaper photo captured us:
Dad and Mom poised to lead,
my brother with trumpet,
my sister at the piano,
me with pencils—
unwilling to pose,
unsure how I fit.

His first stand was voting rights.
"We urge the state,
the counties,
the local governments
to emphasize voter registration—
without discrimination,
without intimidation."

Plain words.
A sharp reminder:
democracy meant little
if fear still guarded the ballot box.

As Executive Director,
he was called to Washington—
consultant to the US Public Health Service.
Not a new call,
just reshaped.
He had prayed at bedsides,
walked factory floors,
shared suppers with the poor.
Now it was clean air, safe water,
equity before charity—
the same gospel,
spoken in a different sanctuary.

In Virginia, schools were next.
At the Governor's Conference on Education,
he weighed the gaps.
Reports boasted of "11 percent Negro enrollment"—
the official language of the time,
already heavy with its own history.
He called it plain—misleading.
"Forty percent of Negro students
were leaving before graduation."

"By their actions," he said,
"the white power structure is satisfied
to continue this injustice—
to keep the Negro in his place."

He pressed further: textbooks.
"Who decided to eliminate
stories favorable to Negroes?"
Benjamin Banneker—erased.
Slave trade evils—gone.
Negro boy saving white boy—deleted.

What children read,
and what they were kept from reading,
was its own lesson.

Behind the scenes:
clipping service stacks—cross burnings,
rallies, hate mail.
He filed them all.
Evidence that silence was complicity.

He traveled the state,
spoke in councils,
stood where a church had burned,

sent reports on Klan activity.
"It is my prayer—and my determination—
as long as there is breath in my body,
to work for good human relations in Virginia—
Negro and white together."

The word fit the era's tongue,
though the weight behind it
was already pressing toward change.
Some called it progress;
others found new ways to hide the old lines.

Dad uncovered businesses dodging the Civil Rights Act—
turning cafés into "private clubs,"
beaches into "members-only" shores,
and justice into something
you had to buy a membership for.

At home we learned new habits:
locked doors,
drawn blinds,
basement play
while storms pressed the glass.

That summer, Granddaddy Combs died—
a heart attack in his chair.
But Grandmother blamed Dad's work.
Said his voice had broken her husband's heart.
The last thread between them snapped.

Kindergarten: J. E. B. Stuart Elementary.
I didn't know the name
was carved in Confederate stone,
or that my great-great-grandfather
had marched to Stuart's orders—
boots in the red Virginia dust,
following a cause he couldn't question.

Didn't yet understand
what it meant to be the white boy who stayed
when others fled.
But I felt it—
the stares,
the questions.

Am I Black or White? I asked Mom.

Crosses burned in the front yard.
Hate mail stacked like kindling.
Lee bore the worst—
chairs kicked, books thrown.
He found a shield in friends,
Black and white together.

Pam turned to music.
Her violin steadied her,
an orchestra of friends,
each note a refuge,
harmony rare outside those halls.

Mom led the PTA,
sat at the piano to teach,
showed strength could be sung
as well as spoken.

And me—
I played,
skinned knees,
slowly learning the world had edges,
some drawn by design.

Dad pressed on.
Council chambers, country churches,

Freedom Rallies on courthouse steps.
His words carried prayer:
Black and white together,
shoulder to shoulder,
not divided by fear,
but united in faith—
"one Virginia,
one nation,
under God."

Mom pressed on too—
maps in her lap,
hands on our shoulders,
compass without pulpit.

But hate seeped in.
Even inside the Council—
a staffer smiled,
then betrayed,
leaking our lives to the Klan.

We didn't know it yet.
The storm was circling,
closing in.
We were still reading the chapter,
line by line,
while the light thinned at the edges.
Not gone.
Not yet.

6

Creosote and Color TV

Support was thinning like old paper.
Opposition?
No longer in hoods—
now in neckties and name tags.

And he stood in front of them.
Not hidden,
not hedging,
but calling them by name—
naming the power they held,
naming the cost it carried.

Dad still got telegrams from Humphrey—
a quiet nod from Washington.
But in Richmond,
doors closed softly,
pulpits sidestepped,
allies slipped into silence.

On Sundays,
he and my brother drove past Klan rallies,
scribbling license plates like roll call.
Hate wasn't hiding anymore—
it was standing proud
on courthouse steps.

Mom fought her own way—
knocking on doors
where she wasn't welcome.
Met with slurs, guns, slammed doors.
"Fiddlesticks" was her only curse,
but she made it thunder.

Back home,
the neighbors were kinder.
We built snow forts.
Dad stood in as the snowman,
laughing as if the world itself
could still be shaped by our hands.

But tension pressed in daily.
Even escape had a return ticket.
Pam left with Aunt Susan,
I tried to follow,
was pulled back.
But, Pam didn't stay gone long.

Dad was getting noticed—
too noticed.
He called out Virginia's politicians,
the misuse of tax dollars
spent to fight against civil rights.
"Vote the bigots out," he said,
plain as a headline.

He was asking "Jim Crow" kind of questions—
the kind that stirred hearts in some,
and hornets' nests in others.

The price of his words
came one night:
marbles through our storm door,

while we watched our first color TV.
The future glowing,
hate slipping through the cracks.

He tracked the Klan,
filed photos,
sent reports.
Leaders dismissed them.

Then I found the jar.
Creosote, swastika on the lid,
held fast by the bushes,
branches bending like a shield
that caught what hate had thrown.
Weeks later—another jar,
this one hurled through my sister's window.
Glass glittered,
creosote splattered.

We slept on,
the fan's hum masking hate
with a lullaby thin as glass.

That night marked the divide.
Shadows became proof.
Rumors turned to shards.
And still the question: Why us?
I only half knew.

Mom and Dad had been fighting for fairness,
for doors open,
for every child to belong.

Through a child's eyes I saw it:
the threats were real.
The hate had a name.

And my eyes—
once wide with wonder—
never closed the same again.

7

Leaving with the Wounds

By morning,
detectives stood in our bedroom.
Dark suits.
Heavy silence.
Words no child should overhear.

Dad kept the creosote-stained bedspread—
never washed, never thrown away.
Proof that justice has a cost.

My sister slipped back to her violin.
I clung to Mom in the kitchen doorway.
Something shifted in us.
We were never the same.

At night, Dad sat with a shotgun on his lap.
Waiting.
He trained Lee:
woke him in silence,
placed him at the stairs
with pistol and shotgun beside him.
"If someone gets past me," he said,
"you know what to do."
Reassuring him—
"Your mother will come running."

It never came to that.
But fear came close enough.

Then—he resigned.
March 1967.
The silence afterward was louder than hate.
Support had dried up.
Whispers replaced praise.
The governor's farewell was polite—
and hollow.

Weeks later, the numbers told it plain:
Klan membership swelling—
"400 in 1965,
over 4,000 by 1967."
Virginia inched toward compliance.
Defiance flourished anyway.

The fire Dad had warned of
was spreading.

Dallas called.
He said no.
North Carolina instead.
Not ambition,
but refuge.

We packed yellow boxes,
loaded the *Mayflower*,
pointed south.

To me, it was mystery—
a train already in motion,
no whistle, no warning.
All I knew:
we were leaving.

And what we carried
was heavier than any box.

8

A Shaky Bridge Between

We left Richmond behind—
headlines, hate, broken glass—
traded for packed bags, quiet resolve.

I didn't know where we were going.
Only that we couldn't stay.
The city's noise trailed off
like the whistle of a departing train.
We were carried forward,
closer to silence than to schedule.

We rounded the arrowhead monument—
stone reminder of battles past,
an old fort,
threshold to the mountains,
peace and hope in one.

The '67 Pontiac groaned up the curves,
three on the tree,
trees thickened, air cooled.
We crossed a narrow wooden bridge,
water laughing beneath our wheels,
and arrived at church camp.

Still lake.
Unfamiliar voices.
Softball, swimming,
burgers by hymnals.

Dad, Lee, and I bunked in the men's cabin—
smoke thick, poker chips clinking,
card-game laughter drifting past sleep.

This wasn't Richmond.
But it was something next.

Worship in the mess hall,
grits, biscuits and bacon,
fried frog legs and chicken at Sunday lunch.
A different kind of communion.

I stayed close to Mom,
her voice still my compass.
Kindness here was cautious.
Dad listened, shook hands,
a shepherd learning the land.

Then we left the dammed lake
for what would be home:
Sweetwater.

A manse beside the church—
frame houses, red clay,
and here and there a brick one
holding its color against the dust.

Pride wrapped in silence.
Peace with shadows.
Still, we unpacked.
We settled.

9

Where the Dust Settled

We left church camp with dust on our shoes—
seeking rest,
finding a manse that felt like a tavern,
a stopping place that became staying.

Four bedrooms,
space enough to dream.
Walls that carried prayer,
floors steady enough for roots.

Sweetwater spread like a patchwork quilt—
roads and porches bound by red clay.
The land was old, granite-deep.

Sweetwater ran on work-worn hands—
factory shifts, mill dust, farm calluses—
threads pulled tight across income lines,
just to keep the community
from coming apart.

At noon, the quarry thundered;
cracks split the church walls.
Dad measured them,
fought for repair.
The church stood.

So did he.
In time, the blasts softened—
and his first real win
belonged to the whole community.

Mom gathered the church youth,
fed them pizza—
our city favorite, new to their tables.
Discipleship shaped in circles.
Not loaves and fishes,
but warm pies, steaming invitations
to belong.
Some stepped away,
choosing sandwiches at home.
But love has gravity—
and in time,
the circle drew them in.
So did she.

Dad still took us to visit his mother,
even when wounds were raw.
Grandmother gave us odd gifts—
like tickets to *Gone with the Wind*,
as if history could be handed down in Technicolor.
Confederate romance,
magnolias and plantations—
a South painted for the screen,
performed as truth.
I sat in the dark,
watching a version of history
that never matched the stories we lived.

Sweetwater Elementary staged its own version.
All white.
A school stitched into a low-to-mid-income community—
paddles hung in plain sight,

their silence part of the script.
At first, I felt smart.
Then restless.

One day I wasted construction paper.
Five licks.
It wasn't discipline.
It was theater—
punishment performed for an audience,
humiliation masquerading as order.

Mom and Dad resisted that kind of punishment.
But I still watched him hand a PTA award
to the very teacher who bruised my spirit.
Something cracked in me.

Looking back,
maybe Dad was leaning on a soldier's creed—
praise in public, correct in private.
Still, the moment stung.
Recognition wrapped in silence.
Not long after, she retired,
leaving me with questions
no ceremony could mend.

Then the news broke:
Dr. King was gone.
A shot into hope itself.
The color TV turned solemn,
justice cut mid-song.
It shook the house.
It shook my father.
He knew hymns weren't enough.
The streets demanded policy.

Mom carried it too—
not in speeches,
but in classrooms, in PTA halls,
stitching justice into daily bread.

Two instruments,
one unfinished symphony.
His voice carried over crowds—
bold, public, political.
Hers rose beside it,
steady and angelic,
soft but unyielding.

Together they turned outward—
he toward Raleigh and the ballot,
she toward schools and community.
Two fronts. One fight.

Sweetwater offered peace—
but laced with paradox.
A community whispering calm
while the world roared with old rules.

Still—
it was home.

10

PK: Sugar, Sins, and Salamanders

Pain etches deep—
like lightning splitting sky.
Even when you don't want it to,
it leaves its mark.

Preschool meant soap for speaking out,
a ruler for being a kid.
By third grade, paddlings turned public.
Or worse—
the "Little Red Room,"
a red door, a canoe paddle waiting.

What stayed wasn't the sting.
It was the silence.
The shame.
The shy kid clinging to his mother was fading.
A restless spirit was rising.

Our corner of the South was shifting too.
Wallace's name rode bumpers,
coalitions re-formed,
the ground itself seemed to move.

Dad felt it.
He turned toward politics.

Mom was right there,
her questions shaping every conversation.
Faith and politics
became daily bread.

Meanwhile, I roamed Sweetwater.
Sticks for swords,
quarries for castles,
creek beds for thrones.
Salamanders slipped between my fingers—
bright, living jewels of the mud.

The curb market our palace—
Bazooka gum, Baby Ruths,
sugar bought with bottles and scrap.
But temptation came sharper.
Coins from Dad's collection.
Then from the Sunday school office.

I was caught.
Dad didn't yell.
"Return it. Apologize.
Now—go get a hickory."
Not a tree branch,
but a forsythia switch—
thin, green, stinging.

It hurt.
But deeper still—
trust, broken.
Mom explained it plain:
"You didn't take money.
You stole trust."

Even as a kid, I knew what it meant—
how discipline carved deeper than the moment.

My childhood had already translated it for me.
That cut sharper than any switch.

Because I'd heard it in church:
"He that is faithful in that which is least
is faithful also in much:
and he that is unjust in the least
is unjust also in much."
(Luke 16:10 KJV)

And suddenly it wasn't just coins.
It was character.
It was whether I could carry
the smallest responsibilities
before being asked to shoulder larger ones.

Being a PK meant living under a microscope.
Masks I hadn't chosen—
one for church,
one for polls,
one for the classroom.
Never enough room for the boy underneath.

I wanted to be a kid.
Instead, I was also the son of important people.
Every glance carried judgment.

The lesson stuck:
trust can crack like stone,
turn to dust,
a fault line waiting
for the next quake.

And like politics,
when the ground shifts,
no one stands untouched.

The earth was moving—
granite or not—
quarry dust in the air,
feldspar seams beneath us,
in our family,
our state,
in me.

And the truth pressed in:
trying to stand still
on moving plates
isn't safety.
It's surrender.

But even fractured rock
can hold its shape again.
Even shaken trust
can settle back into place.

Mom and Dad kept teaching—
through presence,
through patience,
through quiet corrections I shrugged past.

Only later did I see
their lessons never left;
they waited—
steady as bedrock,
just beneath the surface
of my wandering steps.

II

Scars You Carry, Scars You Hold

We fought wars in pine jungles and red dirt foxholes—
Vietnam, Normandy, the Alamo—
battles played with BB guns and firecrackers,
mimicking someone else's grief.

Vietnam was everywhere:
headlines, haunted eyes,
neighbors who didn't come home.

Dad never glorified war.
He carried his own weight—
letters locked away,
names unsaid.
Our blood had worn uniforms back to the Revolution,
but not every banner was worth following.
Courage without cause—shackles.
Service means freedom for all—
not loyalty in chains.

Mom served too—
not in uniform,
but in song, sweet treats,
and justice stitched into school halls.
On porch steps,
she stared down shotguns,

her voice steady for civil rights.

Real wounds weren't bruises.
They looked like men in fatigues
talking to trees,
laughing too hard at nothing.
Dad didn't flinch.
Presence was prayer enough.

We lived where race jokes
scattered through classrooms
like gravel on pavement—
sharp, thoughtless.
Mascots stitched with rebel flags,
colors mistaken for courage.
"Pointy heads," they said of the Vietnamese—
echoes of a war we didn't fight,
still spilling from young mouths—
fed by a narrative skewing history.

But at home, courage meant quiet.
Not the kind that shouts,
but the kind that steadies.
Power was patience.
Protection, a form of love.

Dad handed my brother a shotgun first.
Then me.
I didn't brace.
The 20-gauge knocked me flat.
He didn't scold.
Just nodded—
"Now you know."

Another Thanksgiving—
I slipped on ice,

my gun hammer splitting my hand.
If it had been cocked . . .
Dad didn't say.
He didn't need to.

He honored guns with boundaries.
Shotguns for food,
pistols for protection—
never swagger.
Restraint was care.

And somewhere in it,
a truth as old as Scripture:
"Power is made perfect in weakness."
Not the force in your hands,
but the strength in knowing
when to hold back.

Mom's line was simpler:
no risk too small,
no child too far.

She once ran to save a toddler
clinging to the bumper of a '57 Chevy.
Not her child,
but hers in that moment.
She didn't weigh danger,
she just ran—
the way the Shepherd leaves the ninety-nine
to gather the one who's lost.
Because to her,
every child was worth the sprint,
every life worth the reach.

Sweetwater stories piled on.
One summer we came back from camp to whispers—

a husband shot by his wife.
A stretcher.
A blood-soaked sheet.
No sirens.
No justice.
Casual ride in an ambulance.
The talk hinted at more—
a silence that finally broke.

We were too young to know many truths,
but old enough to feel its weight.
The family vanished soon after.
No explanation.
No reckoning.
Only absence.

My backyard battles ended.
The real ones stayed—
between pride and humility,
fear and empathy,
privilege and purpose.
Sometimes a wound appeared
the way small cuts do—
sudden, sharp,
no story attached.
But Mom—especially—
was there to bandage it,
to steady the sting,
to remind me healing
was a family practice.

My mom was never loud.
She lived it.
Faith steady.
Justice patient.
Scars were held—

with prayer,
with presence,
with a love that stayed.

12

Rocket Fuel and River Stones

Mom believed in education—
she became it.
Not for acronyms or tassels,
but because learning was survival,
legacy, faith in motion.

At Lenoir-Rhyne she returned,
made the dean's list,
earned her degree—
not for the title,
but the transformation.
Then Appalachian,
where mountains met meaning,
and knowledge stretched
as wide as the ridgelines.

She braided science and Scripture—
sediment became story,
the Big Bang, Genesis in motion.
In her classrooms, truth needed no label—
only light.

At home, Saturdays meant wonder:
quartz, amethyst, emeralds, rubies,
rock tumblers humming like hymns.

The den turned museum,
our shelves heavy with stardust.

Dad loved history the way Mom loved science.
Every battlefield, every placard—
he carried the past like a compass,
lessons buried in stone and story.
To him, every step forward
meant remembering who had walked before.

We loved to travel.
Mom and Dad folded those journeys
into our childhood,
repeating trips to places like
Cherokee and Tweetsie Railroad—
not just for the entertainment,
but for the stories of the people,
the land,
the culture beneath the surface.

Even the car rides became classrooms.
Games in the back seat,
questions from the front,
and long talks about where we were headed
and why it mattered that we knew
what came before us.

Then came 1969.
Apollo 11.
Florida.
A gas station stop—
barefoot, glass, eleven stitches.
Mom's hand gripping mine tight.
Her love stitching more than my foot.
Holding us steady
in a world still divided.

Then Kennedy Space Center.
Rockets towering,
questions bigger than I could hold.
Dad read every word,
his voice threading the moonshot
into Kennedy's promise,
the sweep of history
that carried us here.

Mom glowed like the launchpad,
her wonder lit by science
as if the stars themselves
were whispering back.

We looped through Florida,
all the way to Key West—
the edge of the map.
Then back for the real thing.

July 16. Cape Canaveral.
Hundreds of cars,
radios buzzing, sky wide open.
The rocket roared,
a streak of light rising.
Dad caught it on his 8mm.
Blurry, but enough.

Days later, our color TV
brought the moon home.
A man stepped onto it—
and suddenly we weren't just Sweetwater kids.
We were citizens of the cosmos.

Looking back, I see it now—
the museums, the road trips,

the stitched foot, the gemstone shelves.
They weren't distractions.
They were invitations.

Mom didn't just teach science.
She revealed wonder.
Dad didn't just tell history.
He placed us inside it.

Together they showed us:
faith and curiosity,
memory and vision,
can walk side by side—
hand in hand—
toward the stars.

What once cracked and scattered
can be gathered,
like gemstones tumbled smooth—
their colors distinct,
yet shining together.

Maybe that's what God intended all along:
a society,
a creation,
polished by time and mercy
until our differences refract into beauty.

13

Bobby Lee (Bob): Ballots and Battlefields

Mom and Dad—two paths, one purpose.
She taught science and Sunday school,
saw God in sediment and song.
He stood in pulpits and precincts,
guided by history, anchored in justice.

Dad wrestled with his roots—
railroad men, a mother of open arms,
Confederate portraits, whispers of ownership.
He didn't glorify the past.
He traced it to reckon with it,
to change what needed changing.

He followed in his mother's footsteps.
Grew a new daycare from the church hut—
women from Sweetwater running it,
seeded in faith, watered by love.
Presence, paychecks, purpose—
each act a bridge,
each purpose building a larger table,
wide enough for neighbors,
steady enough for hope.

Service spilled outward—
from cancer crusades to county needs,
faith translated into action.

When he ran for office,
he used his given name: Bobby Lee (Bob).
Friends mocked it (blub, blub).
But he carried it into the campaign.

He crossed lines and tracks—
the kind that divided more than towns.
From the Ridgeview barbershop,
to the mill hill humming with labor,
to back roads where the soil still held its scars—
he traveled them all,
every corner of the district he hoped to serve.

Door by door,
he listened,
earned trust—
steady steps that stitched together
a map of voices
others overlooked.

I tagged along, posters in hand—
symbols heavier than I knew,
promises inked in color,
weight carried mostly by him,
but brushed onto my shoulders too.

The political pot boiled.
Signs sprouted like weeds,
some doors opened, others stayed cold.
Even church pews emptied.
Still—he stayed.
Never campaigned from the pulpit,
but preached justice steady as Jesus.

His platform:
oppose endless busing,
cut waste, fight pollution.
Count childcare as deductions.
Lower the voting age to eighteen.
Protect the right to protest—
sacred when it sought justice,
fragile when misused,
but never worthless.

Mom stood with him—
campaign quiet, classroom steady,
teaching, singing,
her harmony carrying what words could not.

Together they made space—
for neighbors who didn't
look like us,
love like us,
pray like us.
Grace that welcomed.
Faith that didn't flinch.

I didn't see it then—
too caught in school dances and campaign trails.
I see it now:
a father learning from history,
a mother finding God in science,
and a boy—me—
caught between privilege and purpose,
trying to carry a calling
that never let go.

14

What Ashes Left Us

The seventies came fast—
loud, wild, sideways.
Dad leaned into it.
Hickory's Centennial asked every man to grow a beard.
He grew Elvis sideburns instead,
pinned on a button—*Brother of the Brush.*
Half preacher, half politician,
Rock and Roll charm.

Mom's reach was growing too.
Her voice carried through the NCAE—
first local, then state—
shaping policy as surely as she shaped students.

Dad had just won his first election,
North Carolina State Senate.
Not with sound bites,
but with presence—
earned in living rooms,
meeting halls,
long walks through neighborhoods
where justice still felt far off.

He didn't pocket the victory.
Every Senate paycheck

went back into church or charity—
salary turned to seed,
planted in soil deeper than politics.

My own world was smaller.
First crush—
born from a birthday spin-the-bottle game.
Awkward kiss,
heart racing.
Then gone.

Her family's catering shop,
just across the road,
burned to a shell.
No goodbye—
only ash and silence.

In Sweetwater, people vanished like that—
a fire,
an embarrassing moment,
and a family was gone.
No chase,
no follow-up.
Just hush.

Fires became background noise.
Frame shop,
mobile home,
even the elementary school—
burning low at night.
Sirens, smoke,
volunteers fighting flames with grit alone,
but the nights kept catching fire.
No answers.

Sometimes the message was smaller—
eggs splattering our church and house,
yolks sliding down brick
like warnings left to dry.

It wasn't paranoia.
It was preparation.
Learning to live where protest
could be a prayer in motion—
or a target on your back.

Fire ran through our story.
Dad's great-great-grandfather's house burned,
its bricks laid by enslaved hands,
the weight of silence baked into every wall.
The land itself carried shadows—
War of 1812 land grants,
ledgers without full names,
children born in margins,
lineage half remembered,
half denied.

Even those bricks
couldn't stand forever.
Dad taught us:
fire can reveal,
or consume.
The difference is who holds the match.

And like the prophets once said,
God does not leave us in the ashes.
From what is burned,
He can bring beauty.
From what is lost,
He can light the path forward.

In Sweetwater,
we saw both.
Ashes and embers.
But also two steady figures—
Mom planting, Dad rebuilding—
who kept showing us
that even where fire scorched deepest,
love could still take root.

15

Tools in the Box

Even young, I knew how to rebuild—
not from skill,
but from watching them.
Dad swung the hammer,
like Papaw before him—
calloused hands shaping more than wood.
Mom lived compassion.
Every tear worth mending,
every storm outlasted.
They taught:
"Keep more than one tool in your box."

That burned-out catering business—
I scraped boards,
walked beams I had no business on.
Not building,
just being there.
Faith with calluses,
love in motion.

Hickory knew that kind of truth—
a town born from a tavern stop,
grown by rails and wagons,
its craft carved by hard hands.

But not everything lasts.
Even in Sweetwater,
some things slipped away.

Thumper darted after camp.
The speeding car didn't stop.
Fur, gravel, stillness.
Dad dug the grave.
Mom wrapped him in a towel.
No words—only presence.
And Dad never left
until the earth was settled,
until the last shovelful closed the silence.

That was who he was—
care didn't end with breath,
it stayed until the ground itself
said amen.

Sometimes they softened loss
with an open door.
"Pack a bag," they'd say,
and suddenly we were chasing
the latest and greatest along the East Coast.
That year—Walt Disney World,
Thanksgiving,
just after the Mouse opened his doors.
Holy ground wasn't stained glass.
It was family gathered—
joy stretched wide enough
to hold both sorrow and delight.

But wonder never lasted long.
The castle faded,
the monorail gave way to back roads.
And back in Sweetwater,

the air carried a different weight—
smoke, red dirt, pine pollen,
and the rumble of distant blasts.

Gunfire cracked the sky—
sometimes target practice,
sometimes hunting gone careless,
sometimes feuds that never really ended.
One neighbor woman never missed,
unless she meant to—
Hatfield-and-McCoy-ish,
all over a dirt road claim.

And if your bike or motorcycle
strayed too close to someone's land,
shots rang out—
not to hit,
just to scare.

That was Sweetwater.
Wild enough to scar,
true enough to believe.

When tempers rose,
it was Dad who stepped in—
steady voice, open hands,
settling storms before they broke loose.
Not law, not judge—
just presence.
And somehow,
that was enough.

Still—we stayed.
Broken bones. Quiet prayers.
The manse filled with knocks and needs.
Dad steady.

Mom beside him.
One hand on a book,
the other on a broken heart.

We learned:
presence—showing up—was power.
Sweetwater looked quiet,
but quiet isn't always innocent.
Sometimes silence carried strain,
sometimes calm only covered unrest.

And the tools they carried?
Not guns,
not threats,
but hammers and hymns,
open doors, steady words—
the kind of tools
that built more than houses,
that held a community together
when everything else cracked.

Still—
we stayed.
From their firelight,
we learned how not to disappear.
That life is a workshop,
and love the tool
you never put down.

16

Porch Light Prayer and Kitchen Therapy

The hammer and the hymns stayed with us—
echoes of who they were,
lessons carried forward
as the years moved on.

A girlfriend chose me—
then disappeared.
Empty desk.
No note.
Her house leveled
for progress—railroad progress.
Steel and timber—
Hickory's old heartbeat—
still echoing through town.
A switching station
where childhood changed tracks,
and I learned
how easily life reroutes itself.

Steel and gravel marked more than progress.
The rails could carry people forward,
but they also made the line bolder—
poor from wealthy,
Black from white,

me from the girl
who never got to say goodbye.

Sweetwater swallowed people
like footprints in rain—
there one moment,
then blurred,
gone without a trace.

Mom noticed the stare.
Didn't press.
Just asked,
"Want to help me in the kitchen?"
Peeling carrots,
chopping onions—
slow therapy
in a simmering room.

But the kitchen
was only act two.
The first was written in rows—
strawberries leading the way,
cucumbers climbing trellises in the June heat,
tomatoes staked high.
Dad bent to the soil,
Mom to the weeds.
Together they taught
that growth takes tending—
from seed to table.

Their garden was more than food.
It was endurance:
some things grow crooked
but still bear fruit.
Storms come sudden,
but roots can hold.

What you plant in faith
feeds more than the body.

The peeler
peeled my knuckle,
but even pain
folded into practice.
Healing came in rhythm:
chop, stir, taste.
She taught me to speak again—
with flavor,
with fire,
with her.

Dad?
Sometimes no words needed.
Just porch-sitting at dusk,
the garden breathing out its day,
rows darkening into shadow.
Watching the sun drop
behind the steeple—
a prayer without words,
an Amen in stillness.

From those small rituals
came their larger purpose.
Faith was never theory.
It was presence,
action,
a life stitched with meaning.

I watched it in Dad—
not just in gardens or sermons,
but in the quiet way
he handled the heat of public life.
He'd help change the rules—

helped make our school board elected
by the people,
ballots instead of back rooms.

It was meant to give the community a voice.
But when the ballots came back misprinted
in a few precincts,
the whispers started.
Others might have cried fraud,
fanned the fire,
turned doubt into advantage.
Dad didn't.

He bent to the truth
the way he bent to his rows—
patient, steady,
trusting the land
to show what was real.
They looked hard at the mistake,
followed every line of ink,
every precinct record,
until they found a path
everyone could live with.

No shouting.
No shadows.
Just resolution—
clean as a straight furrow
after the stone is lifted.

That's how he led:
not by noise,
but by care.

17

Between Laughter and Legacy

Even Halloween carried meaning—
dry ice fog swirling in church rooms,
a little spook sewn into Scripture.
Christmas plays—Santa suits and shepherds.
Hallelujahs and Easter bunnies,
joy stitched into ministry.

After each Christmas play,
Dad would step into the red suit,
beard never quite straight,
eyes twinkling like the last lights
left glowing on the tree.

He'd travel the back roads
with the Parson of the Hills—
Santa with Scripture,
carrying toys and gospel
to the ridgelines of Appalachia.
They taught us:
laughter could be holy too.

Mom read every word I wrote,
teaching me to trust my voice,
to see the worth in my own words.
She signed me up for an International Culture Club—

books, maps, little treasures from around the world
opening windows I didn't yet know I'd need.

Dad taught me to question—
especially myself—
and to look beneath the surface,
where motive, struggle, and grace
often live in silence.
Both showed me
that absence can speak louder than presence.

She worked in schools and nonprofits,
binding people together.
He moved through campaigns and councils,
weighing budgets,
always troubled
when cuts fell on those who needed most.

Legacy always tugged at him though—
fundraisers in place of BBQs,
champagne instead of sweet tea.
Mom smiled through it,
hair pinned, fur on—
but her eyes said otherwise.

Back when they married,
the manuals spoke only to women—
pages of shoulds and musts.
But Mom refused to live
by someone else's script.
She turned a vow before God
into a shared calling,
a partnership that steadied him,
healed her,
and held the two of them
through every crack that life carved.

I'd grown into a country boy
trying to make sense of a city's undertow.
By day, a senate page—
jacket pressed, words measured,
learning the rules of marble halls.
By afternoon, in the apartment pool—
bleach-bitten cutoffs,
a country kid bobbing in Raleigh water,
unsure which world fit.
My confidence frayed,
but I stayed above the surface.

Raleigh never claimed me.
Hickory still held me—
flaws, grit, and all.

Mom made her own trips to Raleigh—
serving with the state education board.

And me?
I was the Senator's son,
the preacher's kid 2.0,
the teacher's boy—
expected to carry conviction like a banner.
But whose conviction?

The spotlight burned.
Life felt like riding the rails—
switching tracks not by choice,
sometimes carried forward,
sometimes left behind
on platforms I hadn't chosen.

Still—
they returned to steady.
Hammer in his hand,

hymn in hers.
Legacy, they showed me,
was built in laughter,
in presence,
in staying steady
when the world would rather
you disappear into the noise.

Dad didn't usually follow the crowd.
He held a straighter plow line.
While others curved their rows
to catch the sun
or please the neighbors,
Dad followed the land—
the real voices,
the real needs.

And when the line started to wander,
when the pull of politics
tugged the wrong way,
he'd tighten his grip—
tug the reins a little harder,
steady the donkey,
right the course,
make sure the furrow stayed true.

Hope was the measure he planted by,
even when it made the field
a harder one to walk.
Faith, like the rails beneath a train,
didn't always rumble,
but it carried the weight forward.

Their lives reminded me:
you don't need the spotlight
to keep the light burning.

18

Salt, Pepper, and Pistol Pete

Nixon won big.
And in North Carolina, that victory
cost Dad his seat.
It was the first real sign
that national tides could drown local voices.

Even Sunday school wasn't free from it.
One Sunday morning, our teacher asked us
to write down who we supported for governor.
Every kid scribbled the "right" name.
I wrote "Bowles."

He held up my slip,
looked straight at me,
and called me out.
A smirk, a chuckle—
like I didn't understand the world yet.
And I lost—
just like Bowles would lose days later.

My little ballot foreshadowed the real one,
a child's paper slip echoing
the sweep of an election.

Looking back,
why were we casting votes in Sunday school?
Why was loyalty to party
measured in the house of God?

My brother was waging war against the War—
peace signs, protests, long hair.
Mom wasn't quite ready for peace signs—
drawn on my jeans—
but she let me wear the necklace,
my quiet, child-sized dissent.

Dad had his own tensions—
once questioning Nixon,
and America's dance with Russia and China.
But when the Paris Peace Accords were signed,
he celebrated—
not the politics,
but the possibility.
The hope
that maybe the dying
was finally done.

I thought he might have more free time—
maybe to help me sharpen my game
on the red dirt court he'd rigged
from leftover marine plywood
hauled all the way from Norfolk.

Basketball was my game.
Softball circled the edges,
but hoops held my heart.
I was set to be Sweetwater's Pistol Pete—
all grit, no glory,
but I believed.

After school, the usual:
double-decker peanut butter and jelly,
devoured like ritual.
Sticky fingers, full heart.

Softball was our spring jam.
We played at Fairbrook—
a scrubby field shy of the city line.
The sewer plant manager down the road
would swing by in his pickup,
tailgate full of hopefuls.
We were trophies in motion—
dented gloves, grass stains,
a little glory in every run home.

Dad—stayed close by.
In the stands,
on the sidelines,
mowing the field next door
just so we'd have a place to practice.

He even helped start a church team:
Sweetwater Presbyterian Softball.
SP stitched on our hats.
We joked it stood for "Salt and Pepper"—
not for race,
but for how wildly our skills varied.
Some launched homers.
Some couldn't catch a cold.
Still, we were all salt—
no pepper touched the ball.

Only rule?
Show up two Sundays per month,
and you earned your spot on the field.
Faith and fastballs.
A theology of teamwork.

I made the elementary basketball team too.
But years before me,
my sister had carved her place—
running the court in a quieter game.

Girls' sports were a different world—
smaller crowds, fewer cheers,
but just as much fire.
She played the Rover position—
always moving,
never left the backcourt,
always overlooked.

Then it was my turn,
we strutted into the gym like we owned it—
swagger without a scouting report,
confidence louder than our layups.

Then came Kenworth.
Just a couple miles down the road,
but a world away.
City kids.
Fast, focused, fluid.
They ran circles around us
like we were nailed to the floor.

That was the first time I tasted reality—
what raw talent looked like,
and how privilege couldn't buy a jump shot.
It stung,
but it planted something deeper—
a seed about race,
about opportunity,
about seeing sports
for what it really was.

Dad kept building his own legacy—
American Cancer Society,
local programs to state committees.
At a national conference in Atlanta,
he stood among leaders,
greeted by Julie Nixon Eisenhower.
He chaired the Governor's Cancer Commission,
pushing for survival,
for human values.

Cancer was more than policy.
It was ministry.
A calling to walk alongside the fight,
to carry the weight
when cure was out of reach,
when faith meant simply
not leaving the room.
To sit with families
as Christ once sat with the grieving,
to pray with presence
when no words would do.

Mom lived it too—
through classrooms and science labs,
teaching children how the body worked,
how cells carried both promise and risk.
She leaned into knowledge
to light the path for others,
long before her own shadows appeared.

Their presence prepared us—
to face what could not be solved,
to stand steady
in the long silence of struggle.

I began to see—
they weren't just different from each other.
They were different
from the noise around us.
Cut from a quieter, deeper cloth.
Salt of the earth.
Light on the hill.

And I wondered
how many hearts
had traded empathy for efficiency—
choosing to move on
instead of truly showing up.

19

Every Task a Signature

Dad never slowed down—
preacher, public servant, landlord, daycare owner.
One job spilled into the next,
purpose fueling purpose.

He fixed up rentals on Grandma's street—
cracked walls, crooked trim,
each repair giving dignity back.
At the daycares, he was the handyman too—
plumbing, painting, adding to the playground.
He worked like it was prayer,
quietly patching the world,
each nail driven not for applause,
but to steady the journey forward.

Campaign season came again.
Signs stapled to poles,
propped in yards,
orange stickers on bumpers,
miles stacked behind us—
rec centers, civic halls,
storefront porches, mill gates.
Ads filling the radio airways.
His campaign was more than politics—
a pilgrimage across the district,

a circuit of faith and grit,
every stop another verse
in the gospel of service.

Mom's hands stitched the same lesson.
She sewed clothes when we were small,
patched the knees of jeans
when we were older,
cut and hemmed curtains
for the home and Sunday school rooms.
Drawers of Butterick, McCall's, Simplicity—
patterns measured twice,
thread pulled tight.
Her sewing was its own sermon:
don't waste, don't quit,
make something whole again.

And her work didn't stop with the classroom.
Community groups, PTA meetings,
her teaching that stretched past the bell—
more than a full day's work.

Add to it Sunday school classes,
choir rehearsals,
and she still called Sundays "rest."
Rest for her was the work of worship,
lifting voices, shaping lessons,
turning service into sabbath.

Together they taught us:
every task is a signature.
Each brushstroke, each stitch,
each mile covered—
a mark of who you are,
a testimony in small things.

Between them both,
We learned work can be worship,
and presence itself
the most enduring kind of legacy.

20

Stitched in Thread

My first real job was at the Sweetwater Curb Market—
pumping gas, stocking candy,
and running the register
because the owner said he trusted Dad's name.
I tried to live up to it.
Not just the name,
but the weight behind it.

That summer, Maw-Maw's side gathered—
the Ervin reunion.
Senator Sam's Watergate role
cast a long shadow,
but it also cleared a space.
People were questioning power,
and Dad was rising again.

The '74 election turned his way,
Senate plate back on the car,
his name in the papers,
called once more to serve.
A comeback,
not for glory,
but for purpose.

Once again,
every paycheck he earned in Raleigh
went straight back—
first to the church,
then to charities,
always to projects larger than himself.

Mom's voice grew too—
from the classroom to assistant principal,
from Sunday school rooms
to choir rehearsals.
Her work stretched past the bell,
her faith carried into every note.

For me, it was a new school.
H. M. Arndt—where county schools collided.
Open classrooms, noise without learning.
Mom saw the flaws—
a patchwork sewn quick, not clean.

I saw something else:
kids divided by labels on their jeans.
Some had vacations and certainty.
Others, just hand-me-downs.
I began to notice
how privilege hides in plain sight.

I realized I was learning a filtered history—
different from the one I had lived,
different from the stories I heard from new friends
on the playing field and the gym.

Even in church pews,
the symbols lined up—
American flag, Christian flag, cross in the middle.
Allies, maybe,

but I wondered:
who were we pledging to first?

The Bicentennial was coming,
everything turning red, white, and blue.
I painted my room to match,
hung patriotic curtains with pride.

Dad leaned into the moment—
faith, family, country,
braided together in that order.
Mom read the symbols differently—
like Scripture,
always asking what they meant
beneath the shine.

And me?
I was learning:
privilege doesn't always announce itself.
Sometimes it shows up
stitched in thread,
draped in a flag.

21

Current Through a Wire

Mom was known in the schools—
Outstanding Elementary Teachers in America,
recognized for her music,
her science,
her way of making children believe
they could see further than the chalkboard.

Dad held the purse strings—
education always first in a balanced budget.
Teachers knew my last name,
and I knew what that meant.
Their presence moved quiet but steady,
through classrooms and council halls,
like current through a wire.

She tried to pull the music out of me.
I stumbled through trumpet,
then sax,
while her melody never faltered.
Choirs, theater, rehearsals late into the night—
she carried beauty forward,
one voice at a time.

Parades were Dad's stage.
The big one—the Soldiers Reunion—

marched through the county seat each fall,
a procession of flags, bands,
and borrowed convertibles.
He'd borrow one too—
wave like a statesman,
retell the family story:
a Confederate ancestor,
marked AWOL,
losing a leg at Chancellorsville,
rescued in a Union hospital.

He never told it for glory.
He told it for the irony—
that survival came from the other side.
Paperwork doesn't pick a cause.
History isn't for worship.
It's something you wrestle,
something that shapes you,
something that wakes you up.

Mom balanced that weight
with her own inheritance—
not relics of war,
but habits of wonder,
connections to the earth.
A microscope as Scripture,
a hymn rising from kitchen to classroom,
showing that creation itself
was a lesson worth learning.

Together,
they carried two different legacies—
his, tangled in history,
hers, stitched with light.
And in the middle,
we were raised to live between them:

to question,
to hope,
to keep the current moving forward.

But the noise outside
too often drowned the harmony within.

22

Broken Rhythm, Steady Hands

Basketball felt like destiny.
Dad once wore #99—
"Hot shit," he'd grin,
"the other guy said so."
I carried that same grit,
NCSU championship pride stitched into me.

Then came the fall.
PE free day.
Jeans, concrete, pea pebbles, a bad jump.
My kneecap slid into my thigh—
pain like thunder breaking bone.
Dad rushed me to Frye.
Surgery, then the surprise:
high blood pressure,
a family signature I hadn't expected.

Recovery was slow.
Wicker wheelchairs,
freight elevators,
girls pushing me like royalty—
I smiled, but inside I was wrecked.

At Awards Day,
I hobbled forward on crutches—

each step across the gym
like a slow walk along the tracks,
unsure if the rhythm
would ever come back.

They handed me a basketball award,
and even "Best Looking."
Pity maybe?
Dad's proud smile steadied me,
as if he saw something
I no longer believed in myself.

From that point on,
sports flailed.
Music too.
The rhythm broke,
leaving too much room
for distraction.
Mom and Dad tried to hold me steady
while steadying the train itself—
keeping us on the rails
when my own wheels slipped.

The rest of the family
was already pulling forward.
Pam had just married—
the Pontiac Tempest—
rolling out of the driveway,
new roads ahead of her.
Lee was grinding toward his master's,
but still back home in the summer—
a coach car attached and steady,
close enough to keep the line strong.

And me—
crippled momentum,

waiting on a signal
that felt slow to change.
But still linked,
still pulled along
by their faith and presence.

Mom's steadiness had been forged long before—
in dawn milkings on her father's dairy farm.
That discipline became her rhythm:
up early, steady schedule,
lessons planned, choirs rehearsed,
the same patience she once saw
in her father's careful hands.

Her strength wasn't loud.
It was daily, dependable,
the kind that held a family upright
when one of us stumbled.

It was in our blood, after all—
railroad men before us laying steel,
farmers rising before sunup,
their grit passed forward.

Now Dad and Mom carried the line—
their presence the engine,
their faith the fuel,
their steadiness the track beneath us.
They pulled more than their share,
so the rest of us could keep moving forward.

Dad's politics carried the same rhythm—
small things that mattered,
order that saved lives.
He pushed a bill on vandalized stop signs.
Friends laughed.

He didn't.
He knew the cost—
lives lost in silence
at an empty crossing.
So he acted quietly,
steady as ever,
a man ahead of his time.

That was them.
Teaching without fanfare.
Writing their own timetable—
with faith,
with compassion,
with hands steady enough
to hold a family
and a community,
at the same time.

23

Some Things Never Change

Dad won the seat again—
took the District,
while Carter took the White House.
Hunt took the Governorship,
a wave of change,
or so it seemed.

Sweetwater stayed what it had always been—
an island surrounded by progress,
never annexed,
never fully claimed.
The city pressed in on all sides,
but its borders bent around us.
We got chlorinated water,
took out the sweet,
but no real growth.
Just limbo—
caught between county lines and city maps,
no one sure who would answer
when the sirens called.

Dad stood in the gap—
vice chair of transportation,
straightening curves,
lowering speed limits,

slowing drag races at midnight.
Progress, they called it.
At least on paper.
But more effort went into
passing through Sweetwater
than ever went into making it a stop.

Highway bridges rose,
but not the kind that connect communities.
On one side—shopping centers, hotels.
On the other—quarry dust and patched roofs.
The crossings smoothed,
not for staying,
but to make it easier
to get to the other side.

Dad dreamed of building
a new Presbyterian church
out toward Springs Road,
near Section House Road—
closer to where families were settling.
"Go to them," he said.
"Faith should meet people where they live."

But the vision fell flat—
met with polite nods,
the safety of familiar walls.
And now, at that corner,
commerce won,
where he once imagined church communion.

You wonder sometimes
what serves a people more:
comfort poured into habit,
or conviction poured into action.

My brother joined Dad in Raleigh—
a milestone in loafers and paperwork,
our name echoing louder
in the Senate halls.

I had played campaign manager,
tagging along at rallies and fairs.
Constituents shook my hand
as if it meant something.
I nodded back,
smelling diesel and popcorn,
learning how policy was a ride
and how change took root
in whispers and handshakes.

Later, I returned as a governor's page—
in agriculture,
representing Jim Hunt,
learning how law grew from soil,
sprouting slow,
rooted deep.

For a while,
I thought I'd study forestry—
trees made sense,
roots told truth.
Maybe it was Mom's doing—
her love of wild things,
the quiet patience of gardens,
the way she listened
to what grew in silence.

Dad saw the potential,
said I'd always been one
to find life in what others overlooked.

I was there to witness—
Dad carrying groceries to the Senate floor,
arguing for open dating,
expiration labels clear as day.
No secret codes,
no hidden shelf life.
He called it truth in packaging—
a safeguard wrapped in plastic.

Lobbyists killed it,
but time proved him right.
Quiet progress came later,
seeded by his insistence.

His Wildlife Committee work
was wilder still.
Parking lot arguments,
civic club debates
where policy was scribbled on napkins.
One man shook his finger and shouted,
"You can f*** my wife,
but don't f*** with my coon dogs."
Not quite the order of business
you'd find in any church bulletin.

Through it all,
Dad kept steady—
choosing integrity
when easy deals beckoned.
For him, even the smallest bill—
a stop sign, a safety code,
an expiration date—
was about lives spared,
truth made plain,
justice met in the ordinary.

Meanwhile, I was chasing the spotlight.
Newspaper clippings circled in pen,
governor's page photos clipped and saved.
On the surface—arrival.
But beneath it,
beer before games,
moonshine "experiments,"
performing adulthood
without the script.

The local paper
tucked Dad's name
between Bridge Tips and box scores,
his work reduced to a footnote.
Still, I circled my name like it mattered.
Like ink was proof
that I had arrived.

Something was coming.
Not punishment.
Not quite grace.
The next page waiting,
a reminder that you turn it gently,
or risk tearing the whole book in two.

24

The Edge of the Wake

River Ridge Run was our retreat,
and their dream of a future retirement.
The manse, our anchor.
Mom planted values like she planted rows—
protect the land,
keep the water clear.
Dad found stillness in fishing.
Mom found it in books and boundaries.
I chased adrenaline—
big wakes, fast boats,
skimming across glassy water
like time could be outrun.

The RRR equestrian shows began with promise,
all grace and polish,
but slipped toward rodeo—
louder, rougher,
wild parties replacing community.
Dad rallied neighbors,
steadying what could be steadied,
keeping River Ridge
from sinking beneath its own privilege.

Sixteen meant risk.
Postgame pizza and beer,

brown-bagging at the disco,
no IDs needed,
as if rules didn't apply
so long as we smiled wide enough.

Dad sat on the Alcohol Control Committee—
his rules brushing up
against my recklessness—
clearing a path for better control
and tax revenue.
Mom's lamp stayed lit late,
her only question, "Are you okay?"
Somehow, that landed hardest.

Sweetwater faced its own test.
A new trailer park—
same soil,
same sky—
met with fear,
not welcome.
That's when I began to see—
privilege isn't something you feel
until you notice
who's denied it.

I stepped out of their careful footsteps
and onto thin ice.
I faltered often,
slipped more than I stood,
and only later understood
how their steadiness
kept me from sinking.
Faith wasn't the rock under my feet then—
it was the hand that pulled me up,
time and again,
until I learned how to stand.

I drove a school bus,
carrying children along the route
through a community shifting.
Sweetwater Elementary changed—
new faces, new accents.
St. Stephens too—
a few Black students,
confident, rightful,
and most kids adjusted quicker
than the grown-ups.
We were the current,
bending with the river's turns,
while the adults built dams
to slow the flow.

When your parents live public lives,
you inherit more than a name.
You carry the shadow,
the spotlight,
the expectation.
Mom gave me her conscience.
Dad, his conviction.
And somewhere in between,
I began—slowly—
to grow up.

25

Stillness After the Blast

At school, we staged the "Mr. St. Stephens Pageant."
Boys in dresses, lipstick smudged,
heels wobbling like the times themselves.
It was laughter on the surface—
but beneath it, a storm gathered.

That storm broke at home.
Equal Rights Amendment.
Three words that split the state—
and cracked our ground.
Every voice inside our house leaned yes.
But Dad's district spoke four to one against.
And he carried their weight.
A pledge.
A promise.
He voted no.

Before the floor vote,
the pressure came hard.
Governor Hunt pressed.
President Carter called.
Then Rosalynn.
Dad later confessed,
"I put my head down—and cried.
It was the President."

The calls kept coming.
Lt. Governor Jimmy Green decided—
enough was enough.
He ordered the sergeant at arms
not to let Combs leave the Senate floor.
No more phone calls.
No more appeals.
Just the vote.

And when it came—
the "no" crowd still doubted him,
the "yes" crowd never forgave.
He was left in no-man's-land,
a servant of his district,
stranded between tides.

Mom had urged yes.
"Justice isn't pie," she said.
"It doesn't run out if women get a slice."
But Grandmother's gospel—
boys at the head of the table,
girls clearing it away—
still pressed heavy in Dad's memory.
Her shadow longer than even Hunt's.

The prophets of politics misread the times.
Dad among them.
What looked like loyalty
became loss.
What felt like caution
proved costly.

Mom bore it differently.
She didn't shout.
She stood.
Books in hand—

Scripture and science,
side by side.
She built her own table
and opened its edges.

Lee was shifting too—
political science blooming in him,
its roots reaching toward a future
that would intersect his path
farther down the line.

Dad called it a tide.
Mom called it hope.
And me?
I called it confusing.
I was tracking graduation—
lake parties, beer cans,
a beach trip before college.

While the Senate quaked,
I was already drifting,
not knowing yet
that standing still
while the world moves forward
isn't neutral.
It costs—
momentum,
legacy,
and the trust of voices
waiting to be heard.

26

Curves in the Road

Sweetwater Road was always winding—
claimed when convenient,
ignored when it mattered.
But Mom and Dad stayed rooted.

Dad was still Superman in my young eyes,
American flag waving behind him.
Mom—the Lois Lane who steadied him,
asked the hard questions.
And me—Jimmy Olsen,
camera in hand,
catching headlines,
missing the story underneath.

But even Superman grew tired.
Politics shifted,
district lines split,
and the very people he'd served
turned away.
Governor Hunt urged him on—
told him his voice still mattered,
that service had more pages left.
Dad heard it,
wanted to believe it,
but the ground had already moved.

He didn't quit.
He turned his hands to what was near.
Daycares, rentals,
quiet cracks most folks overlooked.
Patch by patch,
as if the world could be mended
one nail, one board at a time.

His own heart, though,
was faltering.
Fishing became prayer—
sunrise on Lake Hickory,
casting patience wide
while the water steadied his silence.

Mom stepped forward.
Not louder—
firmer.
From classroom to choir loft,
local charities to church halls,
her voice braided
science with Scripture,
arts with faith.

When the Hickory Choral Society formed,
she signed on as a charter member—
steady, sure,
her harmony a thread of hope
woven into the town's new song.

Music wasn't just art to her;
it was ministry, memory, motion—
lifting spirits
when words fell short.

At the same time
she was shaping another kind of vision—
the early stirrings
of the Catawba Science Center.
Where others saw exhibits and experiments,
she saw possibility:
a place where curiosity could root itself,
where young minds might learn to ask
not only what—
but why.

Her days became a symphony of service—
a teacher teaching teachers,
faith braided with civic purpose,
echoing through Hickory's widening heart.

President of Church Women United—
Greater Hickory.
Chair of Operation Right Start.
Leader in the MOD Mother's March.
Gatherer of women in prayer.

Her presence steadied our home
and steadied those around her,
even as Dad's boldness softened
to a quiet hum beneath her song.

They traveled to the mountains—
to see faith painted
into the bones of a chapel wall,
Ben Long's hands turning plaster to prayer,
disciples rising
from pigment and patience.

They carried beauty home,
hung it with care—

a quiet gallery
of grace and light.

And after they were gone,
those pieces found new life
in the Hickory Museum of Art—
their vision shared again,
offered back to the town
that had long been their canvas.

She even reached toward the stars—
NASA's Teacher in Space.
But when his health waned,
she set that dream aside.
No complaint.
Just love.

Through it all,
they taught without preaching:
hard work earns its keep.
Faith holds,
even when your heart doesn't.
Some things run deep—
blood, love,
the way you keep showing up
when it isn't easy.
Like the psalmist's tree planted by water,
their roots reached deeper
than the season's storms.

And though I stumbled,
their steady presence
reminded me—
grace doesn't vanish
when strength runs out.
They didn't say it.

They lived it.
Steady,
like roots in red clay.

27

Their Light Still Leads

It wasn't a fairytale beginning.
Not for them.
They met through debate—
ideas clashing before hands clasped.
Mom, sharp-eyed and steady.
Dad, fire-voiced and justice-bound.
Not sparks, but conviction.

They chose the hard road—
built a life from questions and callings,
Scripture and science,
sermons and schoolbooks.
By the time I arrived,
the world was already spinning.
Dad preached and pushed—
fighting for kids
before most knew
they needed someone in their corner.
Mom taught,
raised,
and rewrote what it meant
to be both faithful
and fiercely educated.

Ours wasn't a quiet house.
It hummed with purpose—
church calls at dawn,
PTA turned policy,
justice passed like salt at dinner.
Dad built coalitions.
Mom built courage.
They didn't just raise us.
They set the standard.
Mom shaped the measure—grace with grit.
Dad made it move—truth in action.

Following them wasn't easy.
Holy fire doesn't coddle.
It demands.
It reveals.
It lights the way—and casts long shadows.
I tried to resist it.
Pushed away—
from pews and politics,
from the weight of their callings,
from the long shadow of expectation.
I wanted my own track,
my own field to claim.

But even in my distance,
their rhythm still found me.
And so, I watched.
Not just what they did,
but how they endured.
Mom stayed.
Rooted deep.
Hands that once pulled weeds and planted rows
turned to tending children and communities.
She loved the earth—
saw God in every blossom,
in harvests gathered and storms weathered.

Her steadiness was soil:
holding, nourishing,
reminding us that growth takes patience.

Dad showed up.
Spoke what mattered.
Left every place better than he found it—
even when what mattered wasn't convenient.
His life ran like rails,
built for movement,
meant to carry others forward.
It wasn't perfect.
It was real.

And now, in their absence,
I feel their light—
not gone,
just waiting to shine through.
Like so many who knew them,
we carry it forward—
not as memory,
but as presence.
Light refracted,
yet never lost.

And maybe that's the track they laid—
rails forged by him,
seeds planted by her.
Steel and soil,
grit and grace.
One kept us steady,
the other pressed us on.
Together they showed us
that even when lines diverge,
faith runs true—
a rhythm steady as a train at dawn,
a promise as patient as the turning of seasons.

Benediction: Between Grace and Grit

Their light lingers.
Their witness remains.
What they lived still speaks.

Keep an open heart.
Let welcome lead your way.
Carry their steady light
into the days ahead—
grace to guide you,
grit to hold you,
and love that echoes on.

Sources and Inspirations

Memory tells one truth; history often tells another. This book stands where the two meet—between recollection and record, between what was felt and what was written. The material shaping these chapters comes from family archives, historical documents, public records, and the voices of those who lived the stories with us. These sources helped memory find its footing in time.

Family and Personal Archives

- Letters, scrapbooks, and journals kept by Bob and Elsie Combs (1948–1985)
- Hunter and Combs family photograph collections
- Speech drafts, sermon notes, service bulletins, and church records from the congregations they faithfully served

Genealogical Records and Family Research

Connections were traced through census records, marriage licenses, and military service documents retrieved through Ancestry.com. These handwritten courthouse entries helped anchor memory to fact, mapping the Combs and Hunter families across generations and state lines.

Historical and Public Sources

- *Hickory Daily Record*, Hickory, NC (1967–1985)
- *Statesville Record and Landmark*, Statesville, NC (1963–1980)
- *Salisbury Post*, Salisbury, NC (1949–1978)
- *News and Observer*, Raleigh, NC (1955–1978)
- *Ledger-Star*, Norfolk, VA (1957–1965)
- *Daily Press*, Newport News, VA (1957–1967)
- *Richmond Times-Dispatch*, Richmond, VA (1965–1967)
- *Roanoke Times*, Roanoke, VA (1965–1967)
- *Danville Register and Bee*, Danville, VA (1965–1967)
- *The Progress-Index*, Petersburg, VA (1965–1967)
- *News Virginian*, Waynesboro, VA (1965–1967)
- *Presbyterian Survey*, Presbyterian Church of the United States (Nov. 1962)
- *North Carolina History of the American Cancer Society*, Dr. Holt McPherson (1976)
- *The Gate*, Wingate College Yearbooks (1948–1950)

Inspirations and Voices

- Hymns and reflections from *The Presbyterian Hymnal* across the decades
- Leadership of the Presbytery of Western North Carolina
- Stories and memories shared by friends, teachers, preachers, and community advocates throughout the Catawba Valley

These sources—like the people they represent—lent truth and texture to what memory began, helping carry forward the voices, values, and moments that shaped this story.

Author Biography

Ray Combs works in the world of healthcare simulation, a place where stories unfold under pressure and each scene is shaped by human choices and quiet drama. Raised in North Carolina from an early age, Combs has devoted his career to community leadership, healthcare simulation, and operations management. His experiences in church leadership within the Presbyterian Church (USA) affirmed his commitment to preserving stories of faith, resilience, and service—work that ultimately inspired this memoir. *Between Grace and Grit* is his first book.

www.ingramcontent.com/pod-product-compliance
Lightning Source LLC
LaVergne TN
LVHW020638100826
845148LV00012B/2238

* 9 7 9 8 3 8 5 2 7 1 4 1 2 *